T0083774

CITY SCATTERED

CITY
SCATTERED

TYLER MILLS

Cabaret for Four Voices

TUPELO PRESS
North Adams, Massachusetts

City Scattered: Cabaret for Four Voices
Copyright © 2022 Tyler Mills
All rights reserved. Published 2022.

ISBN: 978-1-946482-68-6

COVER PHOTO:
The Mysterious Shine of the Disco Ball,
iStock.com/photo by Suteishi Burusu.

*Cover and text designed and composed
in Mrs. Eaves and Dante by Dede Cummings.*

Other than brief excerpts for reviews and commentaries, no
part of this book may be reproduced by any means without
permission of the publisher. Please address requests for reprint
permission or for course-adoption discounts to:

TUPELO PRESS
P.O. BOX 1767, NORTH ADAMS, MASSACHUSETTS 01247
(413) 664–9611 / editor@tupelopress.org / www.tupelopress.org

Tupelo Press is an award-winning independent literary press that
publishes fine fiction, nonfiction, and poetry in books that are a
joy to hold as well as read. Tupelo Press is a registered 501(c)(3)
nonprofit organization, and we rely on public support to carry
out our mission of publishing extraordinary work that may be
outside the realm of the large commercial publishers. Financial
donations are welcome and are tax deductible.

CONTENTS

ACKNOWLEDGMENTS

I am grateful to the editors of the following journals where these poems first appeared, at times as earlier versions:

Cimarron Review: "Chorus Played on a Victrola: *The Tormentor Compels the Victim*"

Cincinnati Review: "The Study: *Tiny Catastrophes of Everyday Existence*"

Court Green: "I / Self / Woman in Berlin [I wake, put on a silk slip, a wool skirt, and cut]," "Chorus Played on a Victrola: *Every Postcard Carries its Outgoing Stamp*," "The Study: *Resemblance*," "Chorus Played on a Victrola: *Treetop Calm*," and "Coda: *More than Any Film*"

Diode: "I / Self / Woman in Berlin [If you ask me later if I knew]"

Grand: "Interlocutor: *Seen*"

Guesthouse: "I / Self / Woman in Berlin [I saw two doves today. They became tricks]", "Chorus Played on a Victrola: *Arousal*", and "The Study: *The Delicate Language of Signs*"

Pleiades: "I / Self / Woman in Berlin [Cigarette smoke   My lips on]" and "I / Self / Woman in Berlin [Lines and lines of men in trench coats]"

Pulpmouth: "Chorus Played on a Victrola: Music," "Interlocutor: *What This Study Ignores*," "I / Self / Woman in Berlin" [Children build pyramids with bricks]," and "Interlocutor: *Historical*"

Seneca Review: "I / Self / Woman in Berlin [Lindens rain gold moons]" and "I / Self / Woman in Berlin [A spotlight blackens the brick wall]"

TAB: A Journal of Poetry and Poetics: "The Study: *Wealth Doesn't Attract Me*" and "The Study: *Flight from Image is Flight from Death*"

Thank you to Tupelo Press for bringing this book into the world— Jeffrey Levine, Kristina Marie Darling, David Rossitter, and team— and to Dede Cummings for its beautiful design. Endless gratitude and admiration to Cole Swensen for your judge's citation, as well as to Major Jackson, Zach Savich, and Terese Svoboda for your words. Thank you so much.

This book wouldn't exist without the incredible "Berlin Metropolis: 1918-1933" exhibit at the Neue Galerie New York.

I'm also very grateful for the time and space that the Ragdale Foundation and the Doel Reed Center for the Arts afforded while I finished this book. Thank you as well to the Bread Loaf Writers' Conference and the Women's International Study Center.

And thank you to all of the people who were part of this book's journey: Shara McCallum, Carol Moldaw, Jordan Young, Lauren Fath, Peter Buchanan, Renee Buchanan, Donna Woodford-Gormley, Lynn Melnick, Hadara Bar-Nadav, Srikanth (Chicu) Reddy, Lucy

Biederman, Corinna McClanahan Schroeder, David Baker, Kendra DeColo, Jenn Hawe, Elizabeth Jacobson, Jenny George, Vievee Francis, Michael Collier, Rebecca Morgan Frank, Sarah Sillin, Tom March, Susan Steinberg, Sarah Beth Childers, Anne Mason-Jezek, Daphny Maman, Sarah Garonce, and, in memoriam, Stanley Plumly.

Thank you to the Writing Institute at Sarah Lawrence College and the Provincetown Fine Arts Work Center's 24PearlStreet.

Thank you, Arik and Josie, for your laughter and light. Thank you to my family and friends. This book is dedicated to my fellow poets as we sing into impossible places, listening for the voice that comes back from the void.

The "new woman," resented by conservative forces for the
independence that her wage labor earned her and vilified
for being self-serving, promiscuous, and unmotherly, was
nevertheless the darling of a new consumer culture.

—The Politics of Fertility in Twentieth-Century
Berlin, Annette F. Timm

Nor should I on any account fail to mention my many
conversations with employees themselves.

—The Salaried Masses: Duty and Distraction in
Weimar Germany, an ethnography by
Siegfried Kracauer (1930)

Voices:

I / Self / Woman in Berlin

Chorus

The Study

Interlocutor

I / Self / Woman in Berlin

1930

I wake, put on a silk slip, a wool skirt, and cut

past the building bombed to rubble

in the war. Ruin sculpts the air,

moth holed, like the medieval castle

without a roof I played in as a girl.

The treasury prints more paper.

My purse thickens. I sit at a table

and type—and last night's gin

tastes like mulberries on my tongue.

My pulse at my temple flickers

like a copper butterfly,

and the moist morning

feels like another mouth—her

lips startling the back of my neck.

Chorus Played on a Victrola: *Every Postcard Carries its Outgoing Stamp*

One of my friends is pregnant.

They deny it.   *The men.*   *The boys.*

Deny.

What floats on the surface of this?

*

I begin singing in a passable voice
        breaking out of my cage—

the question is whether the image catches reality,
something creative.

*

We come to the city in search of adventure and roam
like comets   with our small incomes.

*

I run away   in my beret with the little point on top.

*

After closing time   at home in my furnished room
I gulp down strong coffee then   *off and away—*

I / Self / Woman in Berlin

1930

Cigarette smoke   My lips on

her lips   Feathers falling

from the stage   My lips on

his lips   My lips on   her

lips on   him   them

These my trousers   This my pocket

This cap, my tie,   my cane

This my dance   This my clock

My tongue   My touch   My eye

My sleeve   My celluloid slide

buckle   My collar   My skirt

My burn   My heart   My bite

The Study: *Tiny Catastrophes of Everyday Existence*

I acquired insight
      in front of a long, raised table
where three judges reached their decision at once
      like meteorologists studying the weather.

Thanks to the question-and-answer game
      a notebook comes to light—
a few heretical jottings
      like victims washed ashore.

We must rid ourselves the delusion
      major events determine a person.
Private feelings   the inner architecture
      of bourgeois ruin.

A woman buys shoes in a large store.
      She recounted to me

           her involuntary wanderings.

Chorus Played on a Victrola: *Music*

      I type
faster and faster.

      A girl
from high

        school.
I used

        to stumble
through

        etudes at
home on

        the piano.
The rotation

        speed of
the record

        gradually
increasing.

Faster   and—
      and faster:

my feet
      stamping

through
      grass.

The Study: *The Delicate Language of Signs*

But the real power of light is presence.

    It alienates you from the flesh, casts you

a costume

    the setting sun, prairie landscapes,

and cowboy songs might never manage.

    The world is not as it is   but as it appears—

the splendid view of the city by night   star-spangled

    like denial.   In the window of one store,

mannequin dolls pose

    in petalled clothes among the orchids.

Do not lean out

    someone wrote across the window.

I / Self / Woman in Berlin

1930

Lines and lines of men in trench coats

ripped at the shoulder

splattered with mud at the hem

lean against the walls

waiting for Unemployment to open

with marks in their pockets

losing value as the shadows shift.

I punch my time at the office,

count each month's days of blood,

fight the manager

sliding his fingers

in & he says do I like

going up, up, up,

gags me,

and the wives of these men

look straight out into the street

as though the wind would create

a new morning,

and I throw myself

into the current—

not lucky, not lucky.

Chorus Played on a Victrola: *Arousal*

I try to learn magical properties

to open the gates   "nice"   "friendly"

like an actress who portrays elegant

villains

How shall I become beautiful   in a suit

morally   crystallized

from the former

inchoate human mass

Interlocutor: *What This Study Ignores*

The study ignores coal staining the sheets

    like ink as they hang out the window,

twisting in the wind down the brick wall.

    Bitters swirl into a goblet in the club

where office workers dance

    after filing paper all day while their

personalities waited outside like bicycles.

    This study ignores the bubble

that formed around them all

    like the shell of a golden egg. And how

can one do an ethnography when

    the word wraps like string

around the tissue of the intestine

    in the guts of the country? I've stepped

on gold memorial stones in the street

    where mothers & fathers &

aunts & uncles & daughters & sons &

    cousins—

The Study: *Flight from Image is Flight from Death*

The naked body evolves into a symbol.

                    Wash away the dirt—

splendor gone from the cartilage.

                    Numerous people remain faceless.

I dream about canoeing

                    into the nocturnal void.

I / Self / Woman in Berlin

1930

I saw two doves today. They became tricks

in the wind: white like a gum

eraser. I saw a tree enclosed in a wrought-iron

fence. What if it fattens, the trunk,

pressing against the metal? It's ashy branches

bunch up at the sky in shivering bouquets

of green and shimmer as the city wakens

like water shoving through the wreck

of a ship: the pewter cups and spoons,

the bones of the captain at the hull.

At the top, all is calm. From above,

what do you see, birds? I think I am

you some mornings while I stand

back to bricks like now and smoke

for seven minutes and watch the dial

shifting under the glass like one

regiment seen from above, in the mountains.

The Study: *Resemblance*

The fantastic sunset is real.
Red, yellow, and green tints—yes—

A number of women
punch cards and write.

Heaven, what a scheme.
We slip in short breaks for ventilation.

A genuine oleograph is a print
textured to resemble an oil painting—

the whole system,   marvelous.
If you suddenly fall

ill, you said,   *can someone take you-*
r place? Yes.   I

          said *yes.*

I / Self / Woman in Berlin

1930

If you ask me later if I knew

the city scattered its sequins

like starlight over the floors

of the clubs, if the city swallowed

death like the crescent of a melon,

if the city coughed out coal

powder in the swirling eddies

of the sky—the sunset like ostrich

feathers framing the face

of a movie star—I would say

no, no, but if you ask me

if I negotiated my wages

so my fingertips would not touch

the trolley floor when I dropped

my glove and saw the stretched

tongues of the shoes chewed

and stained and gapped at the heel,

so I could buy a hot-cross bun

at lunch though the marks shot up,

though the crust shone like a new coin

and could not be touched by the woman

with my face who waited until the line

brought her to the front, and the dough

smelled like saltwater and milk,

and her hands warmed the paper

worth the same as the dream she

whispered into the hair of her daughter

as she woke her in the lapis lazuli light

the night pulled into the room,

what would you want me

to say? I starched my blouse

and practiced the answers to all

the questions and ribboned my curls

and yes, I bought the knot of bread.

Her eyes tracked the curve

of the curb where pigeons gathered,

and I broke off pieces at my desk

while the sky swallowed everything whole.

The Study: *Wealth Doesn't Attract Me*

I asked her to tell me something
about her life on a train

to the suburbs.
But you can already

find all that in novels,
she said.

I / Self / Woman in Berlin

1930

Lindens rain gold moons

all over my shoes when I break

my left heel in the grate above a drain.

We'll wallpaper the nursery with money,

I overheard someone laugh in the hall.

One of the other girls. The company

picnic, the dance, the tennis match

this weekend and next weekend, the season

warm and windy. In the park, children fly

kites with crossed pencils as bones and wings

of paper money. The sun stencils

the numbers—I think of cross-stitch

holes and of my mother. I think of

autumn and how I will be

paid again late this afternoon.

Chorus Played on a Victrola: *The Tormentor Compels the Victim*

I was dismissed without notice,
lost in the skies

of capital, no longer touched
by life down below.

Could I wear a schoolmaster's beard?
Do I bow down to those above?

Am I a cyclist? Am I in a labyrinth?
I receive instructions and pass them on,

lost in the dark
like the writer of this sentence.

Interlocutor: *Seen*

My shoes became insurance

policies. My panties ripped like unsubsidized

loans from interest. *Panties*, a word I borrowed

from (some) porn. Once, I sat at a table

where we talked about *panties*

appearing in a poem after the word *pink*.

My words are worth a dollar

on Amazon if I put them there,

publish them with a cover I designed myself,

plus a three-part plot that involves

desire as skin getting wet—*getting*, like a credit

card swipe—and this ero-

tica will pay my student loans,

maybe. If it sells. If it's good

enough to fill a glass, then why not

serve it?

I / Self / Woman in Berlin

1930

Children build pyramids with bricks

of cash in the road

but I am safe

my wages roll like the water

coming in

coming in

going out

coming in

Chorus Played on a Victrola: *Treetop Calm*

One glance and the director at once knows

no sound penetrates the room

hardly any papers on the desk

He points to diagrams   colorful networks

of lines to illustrate the whole

I recall the days troops were on the march

the war lost   Light signals

inform visitors at the door whether they should enter

or move on   this treetop calm everywhere

in the higher spheres   We enter a room—

countless booklets   the sum

of functions performed   a virtuoso

I / Self / Woman in Berlin

1930

A spotlight blackens the brick wall

An aura   The lit-up bricks somehow personal

Nipples and areolas   I am a clown

with opium eyes—guess if I am

real   I mean   I am part

of three acrobats   a geometry of bodies

a triangle   Now my mouth shares a string

with another mouth   My eyes punched in

with absinthe   Dust brushed on

Bangs and side part   Part shaved   Unshaved

arms raised   I am part   of a line of legs and skirts

kicking up   Spotlight   shadow palms the wall

Empties it   like an   eye

Interlocutor: *Historical*

How can I not talk about what it all means—my mouth

    a sewage grate that takes it all *in*.

Ethnographer, I've caught your voices

    of workers tricked into debt,

into waves of it that shuffle like paper

    lightly on a desk, and my mind

imprints with death camps, bones,

    ashes of my love's relatives. What can I

say, what can I

    do? Think of a mother's hands

pressed on warm cheeks?

    Of families stolen from time?

Am I the I of a future,

    the I who

wants to return

as a warning? How can I be?

How can I?

What flew

around the shoulders

of the workers, into the stones

in the buildings,

and flies, continues to jet

through the windows,

and erupts? *I — I — I —*

Coda: *More than Any Film*

O, weekend.
A hundred reports

of a factory do not add
to its reality.

Can the city
be reproduced?

Photographs of a hundred
views, the mosaic

of single observations?
I perform

mechanical tasks,
interchangeable,

private. But I am
no less a person.

NOTE

"The Study" and "Chorus" poems, as well as the Coda, borrow language from Siegfried Kracauer's *Salaried Masses,* trans. Quintin Hoare (New York: Verso, 1998), a study of wage labor in Weimar Berlin originally published in 1930.

•

Printed in the USA
CPSIA information can be obtained
at www.ICGtesting.com
LVHW090445041123
763052LV00019B/136

9 781946 482686